The Debt Whisperer

How to Get Out of Debt
And Stay Out of Debt
Without Wrecking Your Life,
Your Credit, or Your Future!

Wallace R. Curiel
TMG Books

THE DEBT WHISPERER™
Published by TMG Books.
ISBN-13: 978-1482307108
ISBN-10: 1482307103
Copyright © 2013 by Wallace R. Curiel.
All rights reserved.

No part of this book may be used or reproduced in any manner whatsoever without written permission except in the case of brief quotations embodied in articles for review.
All questions of a legal, accounting or financial nature should be addressed to an appropriate professional in the field. This book is intended solely for the entertainment of the reader.

Printed in the United States of America.

10 9 8 7 6 5 4 3 2

The Debt Whisperer

This book is dedicated to all those who have found the road to prosperity somewhat bumpy at times...

Preface

*Standing in line marking time,
waiting for the welfare dime,
cause they can't buy a job.
The man in the silk suit hurries by,
as he catches the poor old ladies' eyes,
just for fun he says, "Get a job."*

—lyrics from the song *"The Way It Is"*
By Bruce Hornsby

At one point in my life I was broke, unemployed, and over fifty-thousand dollars in debt. This is not something I am proud of but I tell you this so that you will understand that the information in this book comes from someone who has been there and done that.

I just don't believe the lessons I teach can come from someone who has never faced financial hard times or had to scramble just to pay the rent and keep food on the table.

It's like the rich guy in the lyrics from the Bruce Hornsby song—*those* guys can't really understand because they just do not have the appropriate reservoir of experience from which to draw.

Look *I know* from first-hand experience that money, your finances, can just kind of slip away from you. A little at a time, one month after another, you spend just a little bit more than you make and—boom—all the sudden-like, you're underwater.

But, just like I was also able to get myself into that mess, I was able to dig my way out, as well. In fact, I turned it around to the extent that I have gone on to teach personal financial management in college and even been a personal money coach helping others to right their financial ship in a real hands-on manner.

Been there, done that—like I said! And the first bit of good news I have for you is that you can recover and you can do so without wrecking your life, your credit, or your future. Because, I am telling you, if your debt is keeping you awake at night, your life, your credit, and your future are all on the line!

The wrong set of moves at this juncture will only serve to make the problem that much worse and make your recovery that much more difficult. So, take a deep breath, get comfortable and continue reading to learn the lessons of *The Debt Whisperer*.

Table of Contents

Preface
Page VII

Introduction
Page XI

PART ONE
The Debt Whisperer
Page 17

PART TWO
Going Under
Page 37

PART THREE
Getting Zen
Page 81

PART FOUR
The Road to Dream Street
Page 119

AFTERWORD
Page 153

Introduction

Lots of folks confuse bad management with destiny.

—Ken Hubbard

If the amount of debt you owe is, or is becoming, an issue for you, maybe it will be of some comfort to know that being in debt is not an unavoidable fact of life. The truth is that most people do not have a problem with debt.

Take credit card debt, for example. The media would have you believe that we Americans are awash in a sea of credit card debt. But, in fact, according to the latest figures available from the Federal Reserve:

> The majority of Americans owe nothing to credit card companies;
>
> The median balance of credit card debt among households that carry a balance is $2,200;

And only about 1 in 12 of those households that carry a balance owes more than $9,000.

Those statistics reveal some very good news because if the majority of us can live our lives without debt being a problem for us, then, so can you!

But, hey, be careful out there...the airwaves are full of those companies that want to *help* you. You know, you've seen the TV commercials...they offer to consolidate your debts and lower your interest rates. And, oh, by the way, they are non-profits so, for sure, they have your best interests at heart, right? Wrong!

The truth is that, not only do you not need their help, you can resolve your debt issues better, faster, and cheaper by yourself! I mean, even if they are, as they claim, offering their services out of the goodness of their hearts, they still need to make enough money to finance all those commercials and pay the persons answering their phones and running the company, right?

And I do not need to tell you where the money for all that comes from either, right? Because you know that it comes straight out of the pockets of those people who turn to them for help. The "answer" that they offer is actually way, way too expensive for the service that they actually provide. The real answer, and it is the answer that you can begin to implement today, is in the pages that follow.

At this point, let me tell you up front that sometimes the answer to an overwhelming amount of debt can be bankruptcy—*SOMETIMES*—but not very often and even less so if the root cause of your problem is that you have been spending more than you earn.

And bankruptcy, as well as those companies that offer to consolidate your bills, will wreck your credit and make your financial future much more difficult. And they both are likely to wind up costing you a lot more than the plan in this book—financially and otherwise!

If you are considering bankruptcy, however, don't depend on a lawyer to give you the definitive advice you need to decide whether it is the correct course for you. After all, they are in it for the money not for your financial well-being. I'm not bashing lawyers here but I do want to tell you that they will be advising you from a particular perspective.

If I were in the position of considering bankruptcy, I would first seek counsel from a *fee-only* certified financial planner. You are much more likely to get an impartial assessment of your financial situation by doing so. But, if the answer to too much debt is not bankruptcy or debt consolidation, what is the answer?

Well, the truth is that getting out of debt is more the result of a process than a single act and the process begins when you accept that there is no instant gratitude to be had in your situation—it is going to take some time.

Giving up the search for a quick fix is important because the fact is, when approached in the correct manner, you *should* expect that it will take about as long to climb out of the hole you are in as it took you to dig that hole in the first place.

And it is only from that perspective that you can accept this next piece of advice: Pay the minimum on your credit card bills!

My advice to *pay the minimum* is not only contrary to the majority of financial advice *out there*, it is almost counter-intuitive. In fact, most *so-called* financial gurus would label anyone even proposing such a strategy to be insane, inane, or otherwise out-to-lunch!

But I think that many of those same "gurus" must be in the pocket of the credit card companies or something. I mean, why else would they advise you to send those companies as much as you can, as fast as you can, regardless of the cost to you and your own financial well-being?

Do you really think that there is a Mr. Visa or a MasterCard family anxiously waiting for you to pay your bill so they can put food on the table? Obviously not—so what's the rush? The foundation of my *Pay-the-Minimum* strategy is to enhance <u>your</u> level of financial security—not that of the credit card companies.

And the strategy detailed in this book will actually address the *real* reason why you are in debt in the first place. And that real reason, in almost every case is simply this—you have been spending more than you have been earning.

It has been said that insanity is doing the same thing and expecting different results. If your debt is a problem, you won't solve that problem doing what you have been doing—so, isn't it time to try something different?

The desire to pay the money you owe is an admirable one but those good intentions may not be in your own best interest. Reducing your debt is only one consideration but there are others and some of those absolutely take precedence to focusing on your debt.

Observe due measure, for right timing is in all things the most important factor."

—Hesoid (Greek poet; 700 BC)

I fully understand your wanting to get out of debt as soon as possible but the timing has to be right or it could prove counter-productive to your own financial well-being. Look—you got into debt a little at a time and that is the best way to get out because it is that measured pace that will allow you the financial space you need to address the *actual* cause of your debt—spending more than you earn.

Almost all the other debt-payoff methods out there focus on paying off your debts as quickly as possible, too quickly, really, and that is the problem with them. Do you really have *extra* money to pay on your debts? Is there even such a thing as "extra" money? I think not and, in fact, I think that you and I both know better!

All your money has a job to do and, yes, some of it should, *absolutely*, be earmarked to pay down your debt.

But, if you pay down your debt faster than you are financially positioned to do so, it can result in you, despite all your good intentions, doing more harm than good to your financial situation—in other words, you will only make your financial situation worse!

In the pages that follow, I will make the case for why you should follow my Pay-the-Minimum Plan to pay off your credit cards and other debts. And, if you are already having your doubts, I promise you that it will all make perfect sense to you by the time you finish this book.

So, let's get on with it, shall we?

Part One

The Debt Whisperer

Chapter One

When people first hear that my clients call me The Debt Whisperer, they wonder if it is because I teach them how to talk to money or something. Well...while the world of personal financial management can, at times, seem to have a language all its own, that is not the reason.

The real reason my clients call me The Debt Whisperer is because, when I first discuss the issue of debt with them, they immediately sense that I have lowered the volume on the subject. That is, I do not rail about the evils of debt and it is not the focus of my work with them.

In fact, in the beginning, they often get a little nervous because I actually downplay the importance of paying off their debt. But their anxiety is relieved as our work together continues and, eventually, they come to understand my approach.

And the approach I take, when it comes to addressing debt, is based on my years in the financial trenches. Let me explain...

More often than not, having debt is a sure sign that, in the past, you have spent more than you have earned. And, if the amount you owe is growing every month, then you are continuing to out-spend your income.

Now, let me be clear, I am not one of those who make the case that all debt is *all* bad, quite the contrary. In fact, let me assure you that debt can be something of a financial tool that, when used in a prudent manner, can actually enhance your financial position. For example, assuming debt in the form of a mortgage to finance your house can be a smart financial move.

And, too, sometimes events beyond our control can force us into debt. Medical expenses are the number one example of the kind of unexpected expense that can lead to unavoidable debt. Or, a person might lose their job and, again, be forced to turn to credit and credit cards to meet expenses.

But in this book, I address the kind of debt owed, primarily, on credit cards and other forms of unsecured debt. This kind of debt is the result of only a single source—spending more than you earn. And, because you have made a choice to do that, you also have it within your control to make the choice to stop.

The information I will share with you will make it easier for you to both stop spending more than you earn and to begin paying down your debt.

But the reason some of my clients get nervous when we first begin working together is that I tend to downplay the importance of paying off one's debt. They, on the other hand, were expecting it to be the first issue on the table and the eight-hundred pound Gorilla in the room!

Instead, the first thing I want to know about them is their monthly income, the total of their monthly expenses, and how much they have in savings.

You see, those three numbers, alone, will tell me immediately how financially secure they are. And, if the result of dividing their savings by the total of their monthly expenses does not equal at least six, their debt is not primary financial concern.

Certainly, they will need to keep paying on their debt, of course, but I explain to them why they absolutely should not pay one dollar more than they absolutely have to until they have savings equal to at least six months' worth of living expenses.

Chapter Two

Why do I say that your financial security is more important than how much debt you owe? Because until you have six months' worth of living expenses saved, you are, in fact, living on the financial edge.

And if, while you are exposed in this way, you are to lose your job or otherwise can't work for any reason, you and your family (if you have one) are only a couple of missed paychecks away from homeless and hungry or depending on the kindness of family, friends, or the community.

But, in working with my clients, I have found that when a person has too much credit card debt it is also almost always the case that they have little or no savings—the two simply go hand in hand. I mean, think about it—if you are spending all that you earn and then some, how can there be any money left to save?

And the way you begin to address both issues, too much debt and too little savings, is to get the total of your monthly expenses and other spending below the total of your monthly income.

Debt is only a symptom of the real problem—the real problem is spending more than you earn!

Remember, both your debt and lack of savings is the result of over-spending (spending more than you earn). That being the case, your first concern should not be how you are going to pay off your debt but, rather, how you will reduce your spending to the point that it is less than your income.

By reducing your spending to the point that it is less than your income, you will not only stop your debt from growing, you will also free up money to start building your savings and increase your level of financial security.

Money in the bank equals financial security!

Decreasing your debt and increasing your savings are both important but savings represent your financial security and, so, it is more important that you build your savings than it is to use money you could (and should) be saving to pay more than the minimum amount due on your credit card bills to reduce your debt.

The good news is that almost all of us can cut the total of our regular monthly spending by ten percent or more simply by eliminating unnecessary spending.

And the first step towards eliminating unnecessary spending is to identify it: To learn to recognize unnecessary spending and to get into the mindset of questioning every purchase you make before you make it!

This is a critical move on your part if your debt is growing because by eliminating unnecessary spending you can get the total of your monthly spending below the amount of your monthly income and, so, stop your debt from becoming any larger and making your financial position any worse.

The first step, then, is to document your present financial condition to determine where in your spending you are exceeding your income. It is also during this documentation process that you will first identify opportunities to reduce your spending.

Once you have gotten the total of your monthly expenses and other spending lower than your monthly income, and have built your savings to an amount equal to at least six months of living expenses, then, and only then, will it be the right time to shift your financial focus to paying more than the minimum on your debt.

And the first step in that process will be to change the way you spend. Too much debt is usually a sign of too many credit cards. Your first actual task on the road to becoming debt-free will be to reduce the number of credit cards you have to one. All your other cards will need to go and the one that you keep is to be used only according to the guidelines explained later on in the text.

So, by now it is probably apparent to you that this is not one of those books pushing the popular one-size-fits-all solution of accelerated debt payoff at all costs. Instead, what I tell my clients is that there are more important financial considerations that take priority over debt payoff and the first of those priorities is their financial security. And, what is true for my clients, is just as true for you!

I urge my clients to lower the volume of the internal dialogue people in debt usually have with themselves. If you are in debt, you, too, need to do that because, otherwise, debt will overwhelm that conversation and become the focus of your financial life.

But when you focus on your debt that way, you have, in effect, taken your eyes off the prize—you are making a negative the center of your financial universe. Although we all aspire to live debt-free, can you really afford to make it your number one financial priority before it actually *is* your number one financial priority?

Your debt is only one part of your financial life and you need to keep debt in its place. It is better, I think, to focus on a positive—the growing of your savings. And, as your savings grow, so, too, will your financial security and peace of mind.

Paying down your debt at the cost of building your cash reserves is a very risky proposition. Life happens. It only makes sense, then, to put some money away for a rainy day—even if that means you arrive at the promised land of debt-free Nirvana a little later rather than a little sooner.

Chapter Three

So, your debts should never be the focus of your life. And, certainly, paying off your debts is not as important as your present-day financial security. And, again, if you do not have enough financial liquidity sufficient to pay your bills for at least six months, your financial security is not all that secure.

I have seen other writers make the case that the prudent path to paying off your debts is to pay as much as you can possibly squeeze out of your budget every month. By doing so, they write, you will pay the least amount of interest possible on that debt.

The next thing they do at this point of their argument is to show you how much you will save over the three, four, or five years it will take you to pay off all your debts. But there is that kind of save and, then, there is another kind of save—the kind that actually puts money in the bank.

And what they don't tell you is how much self-discipline and self-denial it takes to follow their "Pay-the-Maximum" plan for year after year after year. Frankly, most of us don't have it in us to stick to that course for as long as will be required.

The other thing the Pay-the-Max Plan fails to address is your present financial reality. People get into debt for a reason and, as I said, debt is only a symptom of their more serious financial issues. And, usually, the most serious financial issue I have found when dealing with clients is a lack of sufficient financial security.

What is financial security? Well, simply put, it is your answer to the following question: How long could you support your present lifestyle and keep the bills paid without a paycheck? Income spent to pay off a debt is gone forever—it will not be there if you need it and like it will be if you save it instead!

If you have no savings, you are, in effect, living paycheck to paycheck. But people lose their jobs or become disabled every day! And it is not the case that you need to lose 100% of your income to be seriously pinched.

If you are living paycheck to paycheck and without savings, you might well be only a couple of months without income from being homeless!

You absolutely need at least six-months of living expenses sitting in a very liquid savings account—just in case!

And, if you don't have it, getting it should be your number one financial priority. But, the thing is, if you have a high amount of credit card debt, the odds are that you also have little or no savings.

Chapter Four

But your financial security is only financial job number one. There are other financial priorities that fall ahead of debt payoff, as well. Certainly, you also need to be saving for retirement and, then, there are your dreams.

There is more to life than just making ends meet. And it is our dreams that help keep us motivated and moving forward. But dreams almost all come with a price tag attached, right? So the question is: If we are maxing out the amount we pay on our credit card bills, where will the money come from to finance our dreams?

So, yes, you absolutely should make room in your budget to make your dreams come true but there is also one more financial dynamic that you need to consider when establishing your debt repayment plan: No money is more valuable than the money you earn today. And it is this aspect of the issue that weighs most heavily in favor of my Pay-the-Minimum Plan.

There are two financial dynamics that affect the value of money and both of those dynamics are based on the same factor. That factor is time and the two dynamics are interest and inflation.

The longer money is earning interest the more compound interest it will earn; conversely, the dollar you earn next year is going to be less valuable than the dollar you will earn next week because of the effect of inflation.

Together those two dynamics mean that it is more prudent to <u>save</u> money today and <u>pay</u> money tomorrow. The sooner you put money away the more time it has to work for you. The more you are able to postpone repaying a debt, the less valuable those dollars used to do so will be due to inflation.

Of course, there are other factors that weigh in, but cash simply makes you that much more financially viable and, the more you have, the greater your financial viability is—period, the end!

Let me make my argument in another way that will convince you of the validity of my Pay-the-Minimum Plan:

Let's say you have spent the last three years paying off all your credit card bills by directing as much money as you could find in your budget towards that end. So, now, here you are, three years later and, although you have no debt, you have no savings, either.

Now, let's say, you become unemployed. You have no debt but, remember, you have no savings, right? Well, guess what?

You still have expenses! And, as the months tick by, your situation becomes more and more dire. Hopefully, you will have some family to fall back on, but who wants that as a financial strategy?

Three months later, you are still unemployed and living in your Mom's basement. Your life, your credit, and your future all wrecked. And, because you had no other source of funds, your credit cards are all maxed out again because you used them to pay living expenses and used cash advances to make the (minimum!) payments.

Now, let's look at what would happen if you lost your job but for the last three years, instead of using that "extra" three hundred dollars a month to pay off your credit card debt, you had saved it instead.

You would have about $12,000 in savings—a three or four month cushion to give you time to find another job or otherwise get back on your feet. You are not reduced to moving back in with your folks and your dignity is retained.

And, remember, that entire time you were still meeting your financial obligations—you were still making payments on your credit cards—but you were also saving money AT THE SAME TIME!

Cash in the bank equals financial viability and financial viability is what is important—not spending more than you can afford to reach some promised land of debt-free nirvana!

Part Two

Going Under

Chapter Five

So, how long would you be able to pay the bills if your income stopped tomorrow?

Look, the list of all the possible individual causes of stress in our lives is long but, for many of us, money problems are at the top of that list and debt at the top of *that* list.

Most of us just sort of assume that more money would be the answer to all our financial worries but, as simple as it seems, more money can actually make matters worse!

You see, if more money was the answer then all our money problems would disappear as our income increased over time. But they don't, do they?

So, how does it happen that we take our money problems with us even as we earn more?

It's because, in the real world, our spending grows right along with our income. In fact, what often happens is that the growth in our spending will actually exceed that of our income and our level of financial security will actually diminish as we earn more! There we are, earning more, but still struggling just to keep up with our spending.

Debt is a big factor in how much stress we experience due to our personal finances and nothing puts you at risk of incurring debt like living right up to the limits of your income. And, when you live like that, you will never be able to save and accumulate a ready cash reserve sufficient to get you through a lengthy financial downturn.

A lack of savings is a sure sign that you are living way too close to the financial edge and it is obviously not a situation conducive to your peace of mind. One cause of financial stress that has reached epidemic proportions in our society is the growing anxiety many of us are experiencing because we know that we are not saving enough to ever retire.

Even if we all had the option of working to our last breath, I doubt many of us will actually want to do so. That being the case, you must save for that time in your life when you will need a source of income to replace the income you now earn by working for a living.

And retirement (financial independence) is only the primary long-term goal of financial planning. A sound financial plan will include several other long-term and short-term financial goals, as well.

We can all acknowledge that just keeping a roof over our head and food on the table is a blessing but there is more to a full life than just making ends meet—our dreams must also be considered in our financial planning if they are ever to be realized.

Whether it's a summer wandering around Europe, a cabin in the mountains, or, simply, one day being able to kiss the rat race goodbye, our dreams almost all come with a price tag attached. But a dream will stay just that, just a dream, unless you have a plan for turning it into reality.

The amount of financial peace of mind you enjoy depends on how secure you feel about your present financial situation, certainly, but the future also plays a role in that equation.

If you are managing to meet today's expenses but you are not saving enough to secure your financial future, a sense of dread in your life is all but inevitable. And, if your dreams are going unaccounted for, you are likely to find yourself living with a sense of hopelessness, as well.

It is often the case that the source of much of our financial discontent is not actually our income but, rather, our spending.

The fact is, most of us spend too much of what we earn to allow for any savings at all, much less enough to both secure the future and finance our dreams. And more and more of us are using credit cards so that we can actually spend more than we earn!

Nothing can increase your level of financial anxiety like using credit cards to prop up your income because you live knowing the day of reckoning will arrive. And, yet, that's exactly what more and more of us are doing.

The damage is largely self-inflicted. I mean, after all, it is not as if someone is forcing any of us to live beyond our means. We do it to ourselves and, as we dig our hole deeper and deeper, we surrender yet another measure of financial peace of mind with every shovel full.

Regardless of how much stress your personal finances are causing you today, there are steps you can take to begin to relieve your anxiety. And not one of those steps will require that you earn more money. You don't need to get a second job or work weekends to achieve greater financial peace of mind because more income is only a quick fix and <u>not</u> the answer in the long-term.

The answer is more savings.

Chapter Six

Too many of us get so caught up in the getting and spending of today that we completely lose sight of tomorrow. But if you do that, eventually, you will arrive at a moment that will be like waking up from any other sort of over-indulgent binge. And, almost always, there will be a price to be paid.

The opposite of financial peace of mind is financial anxiety. Feeling anxious about money is all too common these days. Anxiety is a form of stress but stress is not an entirely bad thing. In fact, stress is a biological self-defense mechanism. We experience stress when we are at risk. Stress can be a signal telling you that a change is in order.

So, the fact is, a little stress is a good thing and totally natural. It keeps us alert and vigilant and that is how we should be when it comes to preserving our financial well-being—alert and vigilant. The fact is that there will never be a time in your life when money will not require your diligent attention.

If your debt is now to the point where it is causing you problems, then you have probably figured out that you will need to manage your money more closely than you have so far.

That realization is an important first step in the right direction. The next step is to understand some basic financial principles that can, in fact, help you to better manage your money so you can begin to attack the real cause of your debt "problem."

Managing our money is something of a mystery to many of us. In fact, I would venture to say that most of us never received the formal education that is necessary to manage our money correctly in all the many facets of our lives where money plays a significant role.

I mean, think about it, if we really knew what we were doing with our money would over one million of us go bankrupt every year? (Almost two-million of us declared personal bankruptcy in 2005, actually!) Would a million and a half of us lose our homes to foreclosure every year?

And get this—issues related to money are cited as the number one cause of divorce in court documents! What does that tell you about how good we are at managing our money?

Money management in America is, basically, a train wreck or a train wreck waiting to happen. Sorry, I don't mean to be depressing but the facts speak for themselves as far as our abilities, on average, to manage our money.

The good news is that fundamentals of sound money management are easy to learn and apply. You can do it! And it all starts with a greater awareness of where your money is going.

One big problem with the way too many of us spend is that we have become detached from the process, that is, a lot of the spending we engage in is done in an almost unconscious state of mind. Money comes and money goes and who knows where, right? We earn it, we spend it, it's gone...but who knows where exactly?

That kind of accounting would spell trouble for a small business (or a business of any size for that matter!) in very short order. And, the fact is, your financial life is just that—a small business.

You see, you have income and expenses, just like a small business; you have the need to borrow for capital improvements and equipment (home renovations and vehicles, for example); and you need to save to invest for the long-term.

But few of us have ever acquired the skills necessary to run a small business—and does it ever show! Millions of us run our financial ship aground every year, year after year—but you can do better!

Chapter Seven

Money you earn today is spent on either yesterday, today, or tomorrow. Few of us ever take the time to think about their income as divided up like that but we should because there are some powerful implications to that statement.

You get your check and some of it is spent in the present to pay for today's expenses. That much is fairly obvious. The rent, light bill, and gas for your car are all examples of money spent in the present on present-day costs of living.

That portion of your income that you put away for the future is put there in anticipation of spending that will take place at some later date. Money you set aside in a retirement account, for example, is put there to fund the spending you will do after you leave the workforce.

Then, there is the money that is taken from today's income to pay for yesterday's spending.

This is the money that goes to pay your debts. Debt from past consumption can be like a ghost that haunts you in the here and now. Other than unemployment, perhaps nothing is less conducive to financial peace of mind than debt.

First let's get clear on what I'm talking about here. Expenditures can be grouped into one of two categories: debt or expense. An expense can be thought of as a cost of living that will never go away. For example, utility bills, gas for your car, and groceries are each an expense.

A debt, on the other hand, is a bill that can be paid off and, when paid off, it goes away. A car loan is one example of a debt and medical bills are another. But the debt that too many of us are most familiar with is credit card bills.

Expenses are a fact of life but debt is not; that is a very important distinction that you need to keep reminding yourself of because nothing other than a bunch of money in the bank will enhance your financial peace of mind in quite the same way as will being debt-free.

And, even though most of us accept debt as if it is an inevitable part of our financial life, it is not! But in our society, getting to debt-free will definitely be a swim against the mainstream.

Now, I know, certain kinds of debt are not necessarily *all* bad. Going into debt in anticipation of a larger, future benefit can be thought of as something of an investment. Student loans, for example, are often considered in this light.

But the money paid on any debt, good or bad, will diminish our present-day resources and, in that sense, has a negative element to it and that is this: The money we spend making payments on our debt is money we cannot otherwise allocate to either the present or the future. So, our debt costs us the opportunity to spend our money more wisely or in some way that we would prefer.

The more present-day income that is used to pay for yesterday's spending the more opportunity we lose. So, it should be fairly obvious to you that the less of our present-day income that goes to pay our debts, the better.

Ideally, we would live debt-free and not spend *any* of our income paying for yesterday's spending but, instead, debt is a real problem for many of us. And a real financial issue for far too many of us is that we carry way too much debt that is of no value, whatsoever.

This kind of debt is easy to spot on a Net Worth Statement but I'm getting ahead of myself here—I address the subject of Net Worth later in the book—so, to continue our discussion at this point, just let me just say that the most negative aspect of the debt that most of us owe is that it is, basically, worthless.

Most debt of this sort—worthless debt—was usually charged to one credit card or another and went to support spending that we really could not afford.

The real problem with credit cards, however, is not that they can be used to "pad" our income but that it is way too easy to simply continue down this same road. No money? No problem! Just whip out the plastic!

It is in this way that we lose control of our finances and, once you begin using credit cards to spend more than you earn, you can find yourself locked into a sort of self-perpetuating cycle.

And, if you allow this cycle to continue for any length of time, you will find the total amount of your worthless debt steadily growing. This scenario is actually a kind of trap that more and more of us are falling into every day.

You see, if you allow the total of your credit card debt to grow, then the monthly total of even the minimum payment required will also grow.

What this means is that your income is, effectively, going down because more of it is being used to pay for yesterday's spending. Now you have even less money than you had before! And, now, you will need to take on even more debt to make up the difference between what you earn and what you spend.

When you find yourself in this situation it can seem like there is no way to keep your debt from growing—it can even seem as if your debt has a life of its own over which you have no control!

Chapter Eight

As bad as that situation is, however, the larger issue is the effect that worthless debt can have on your ability to fund the other two elements of spending—today and tomorrow.

In particular, it is our future that is almost certain to suffer in this situation because, when your income is going down, the least painful of the three pots to dip into is the one labeled, "tomorrow."

You see, what too many people do when faced with mounting debt is…well, they panic. And, then, they actually make matters worse by making the mistake of thinking that the problem is the debt, itself.

And, if they are convinced that the problem is the debt, itself, then, obviously, the sooner you get rid of the debt, the better, right? I mean, that makes sense, doesn't it?

And, aren't there all sorts of financial gurus out there ready to sell you any number of books pushing this or that "get-out-of-debt-NOW" plan? Surely, they must know what they are talking about, right?

But where does the money to pay for those plans come from? Well, usually, it can only come from money that should be going to savings. And what you are left with is a really classic example of robbing Peter to pay Paul.

It is difficult to predict precisely how much money we need to put away today to fund that part of spending earmarked for tomorrow, but most of us just know when we're not saving enough. And you definitely know you will come up short if you are not saving anything at all!

One way to judge your financial position is to think about it in terms of what percentage of your income is going towards each of the three elements of spending—past, present, and future. And, if more than ten percent of your income is being spent on debt other than your mortgage, you could have a problem.

In fact, when the percentage of your income going to debt repayment is above the eight percent range, mortgage lenders will begin to reduce the amount they are willing to loan you.

That is an indication of what lenders think about spending on the past. They realize that, not only is it indicative of a problem today, they know it can be a strong indication of more problems yet to come.

And eight percent, if you think about, will not finance much in the way of debt. If you are earning $40,000 a year, eight percent of that is only about $250 a month. That is less than the amount of the monthly payment on most new car loans.

Increasing savings and decreasing worthless debt are both important to your long-term financial security, but the two are not mutually exclusive. And it would be a mistake to think you can't address the two issues, to some extent, at the same time—you can!

But it is my contention that building your savings is more important than paying off your debt.

Sure, we would all like to be debt-free and that is the ultimate goal of the strategies detailed in this book, but there are other, more important, financial considerations to be weighed in deciding how much of your income you can actually afford to allocate to paying off your debts.

Chapter Nine

First, let me further define worthless debt for you. Debt is either secured or unsecured. A mortgage, for example, is secured by property. If you don't pay your mortgage, you lose your house. A car loan is also a secured loan.

Another aspect of a secured debt is that the object underlying that debt will usually retain some part or all of its initial value.

New cars, for example, depreciate rapidly at first but, then, more gradually. Real estate will usually hold its value and, in fact, will often appreciate (that is, go up in value).

And, even though the debt owed will be listed on the liability side of your Net Worth Statement, the present-day market value of that object will also reflect positively on the assets side of the equation.

At this point, let me define the financial term Net Worth because I just mentioned it for the second time in the book in that last paragraph and it is important that you understand the concept.

Your Net Worth is determined by taking the total value of all your present assets and subtracting from that figure the total of all your present liabilities. Liabilities, for the sake of personal accounting, are usually in the form of debts.

The form on which you enter all the data to arrive at your Net Worth is called a "Balance Sheet." If you want to see what a Balance Sheet looks like, simply search the internet using that term or "Net Worth Statement."

People, often mistakenly, judge the financial condition of others by what they see. But real financial success is not efficiently judged by looking at an individual's level of consumption. An extravagant lifestyle, a luxury car, or a Rolex watch can prove a false indicator. If you want to know someone's actual financial state, simply take look at his or her Balance Sheet.

As I wrote, a Balance Sheet is simply an accounting of someone's assets and liabilities. An asset is any tangible item of value that you own such as the equity in your home or vehicles and including the value of your savings and investments.

Again, a liability is, basically, any debt you owe. When you subtract your liabilities from assets, the bottom line represents your Net Worth.

For example, let's say your home is worth $200,000 but that the balance of the mortgage on it is only $150,000. The net worth of that asset, your home, is its value minus the debt owed on it ($200,000 — $150,000): $50,000.

Now, the ultimate goal of your financial planning does not necessarily need to be a million dollar Net Worth. And, in fact, the bottom line might not actually be the most revealing figure on a Balance Sheet.

A better indicator of someone's financial condition can be the yearly growth in their Net Worth as a percentage of their annual income. What that number reveals is just how closely a person is living to the limits of their income and how much of what they earn they are managing to keep.

The fact is, consumable items, such as cars and jewelry, will usually subtract from an individual's Net Worth. This is because those kinds of consumer goods, the kind that steadily lose value over time, do not add as much to the asset side of the ledger as they cost you on the liability side.

Every time you make a purchase, you are buying something that will either appreciate, that is, go up in value, or depreciate, go down in value. Investments are made with the hope that they will appreciate but it doesn't always happen that way.

Any item you consume in some fashion can be considered to depreciate from the moment it is purchased. Food and clothes are just two examples of depreciating, consumable assets.

Cars are another example of an asset that will begin to depreciate as soon as they are purchased. The value of a new car, in particular, drops like a rock as soon as you drive it off the dealer's lot.

Every time you buy a new car, your Net Worth takes a serious hit. Let's say your Net Worth is $100,000 and you, feeling flush, decide it's time for a new ride. Being the prudent consumer that you are, you don't over reach and, instead, you opt for a more modestly priced mid-level sedan with a price tag of *only* $22,000.

You pay $5,000 down and finance the rest over five years. What is your Net Worth after this transaction? It will be less by ten to twenty-five percent of the cost of the car immediately upon your taking possession of it!

How is that possible, you ask?

That decline in your Net Worth is due to the instantaneous loss of value of that vehicle due to depreciation as it goes from being new—on the dealer's lot—to being used—the instant you become the owner. After all, we all know that used vehicles are not worth as much as new vehicles.

And that is not the end of the hit you will take to your Net Worth when you buy a new car. The State and, sometimes, local taxes will always come directly out of your Net Worth with nothing to offset it on the asset side of your Balance Sheet.

All that money lost, thousands of dollars, in the blink of an eye, and for what? For nothing, really! Can you afford that? And, more importantly, is it cost you want to bear?

The point of saving money is, to a large extent, primarily to grow your Net Worth and thereby increase your financial security but, as you can see, buying a depreciating asset accomplishes just the opposite of that.

Now, will there be times in your financial life when you can afford to take that depreciation hit and that it is also a price you are willing to bear? Well, yes, I would say that there could be such a time. But should you be willing to even consider it before all your other financial ducks are in a row? I think not.

There are seasons to your financial life. And there is a season when you should sow and a season when you can expect to reap. And, these seasons have nothing to do with age, strictly speaking:

A twenty-four year old professional sports star being paid six-million dollars a year can afford to take the hit; a fifty year old CPA with no retirement savings? No way!

On the other hand, real estate, and the home you live in, in particular, is one of the few items you consume (through the utility of providing you with shelter) but that can, and often does, actually appreciate in value over time.

Chapter Ten

In the book, *The Millionaire Next Door*, written by Thomas Stanley and William Danko, there is a handy formula to determine how you are doing in regards to building your Net Worth.

What you do is multiply your age by your present gross income and divide the resultant figure by ten. That amount is, roughly, what your Net Worth should be according to the authors of that book.

For example, an individual who is 50 years of age with an annual gross income of $50,000 should, according to the authors, have a Net Worth of $250,000 [($50,000 x 50)/10].

For the sake of an honest appraisal, when using this formula, you should not include any amount of your assets that were unearned such as by way of an inheritance or any other unearned financial windfall such as lottery winnings (you should be so lucky!).

A: Your Present Net Worth: $ _____

B: Your Present Annual Income: $ _____

C: Your Age: _____

D: (B) x (C)/10: $ _____

After you have run the numbers for yourself, you then compare what you should have (line D) according to that formula to what you actually do have—your actual Net Worth (line A).

If you have more than the formula amount, you have done better than average, but if you have less the question is: what will you do to do better in the future?

And, if you want to do better there is a very simple way to increase the likelihood that you will do better: Studies have shown that it is much more likely that you will grow wealth if you have a plan to do so. So, the question is: Do you have a plan to grow your wealth?

> *"Planning and wealth accumulation are significant correlates even among investors with modest incomes"*
>
> —from *The Millionaire Next Door* by Danko and Thomas

That is what the authors of that book concluded after years and years of studying individuals who had managed, basically, to save themselves rich—that those who have done so simply worked their plan to do so.

This is true, they found, regardless of the level of income and it has been demonstrated by their own studies in this regard that it is possible to build wealth on even a modest income.

> "...the overwhelming determinant of the accumulation of wealth at retirement is simply the choice to save."
>
> —from *Choice, Chance, and Wealth Dispersion at Retirement* by Venti and Wise for the National Bureau of Economic Research.

I don't know how to make it any clearer than that. The foundation of financial security and, even, wealth is saved income—money you earn but don't spend! And the only way to have income available to save is to spend less than you earn.

One of the fundamental rules of sound personal financial management is that you spend less than you earn.

This is so fundamental, you would think it needs no explanation but, in fact, too many of us are spending more than we earn, month in and month out.

And just how much should you be saving, anyway? Well, in order to accomplish just the two basic goals of financial planning, financial security and retirement, you absolutely should be saving at least ten percent of your income. Any less than that simply won't get the job done! And, remember, savings equal security!

In order to do that, that is, in order to spend less than you earn, you will, obviously, need to know how much you earn and how much you spend.

And the best way to track these two numbers, income and expenses, is on a monthly basis because that schedule coincides nicely with how often we receive both our paychecks and our bills.

The monthly accounting of income and expenses is accomplished by filling out a Monthly Income and Expense Statement. And, now that we have covered the topic of Net Worth, it is time to introduce you to the Monthly Income and Expense Statement.

Chapter Eleven

As I am about to describe the process of completing a Monthly Income and Expense Statement (IES), you might be led to believe that doing so is a fairly simple process. After all, the Monthly IES is simply the listing of all your income and expenses.

But as simple as it might seem, however, the first Monthly IES you put together will almost certainly be wrong. You see, if you are like most people, you don't really know how much you are spending every month. Sure, it is easy enough to add up the total of all your monthly bills but there is more, much more, to it than that.

And, yet, the bottom line of your Monthly IES is one of your most important financial indicators—so you will need to get it right, eventually. But even before we go into how to get it right, it won't hurt for you to get a rough idea of how your monthly income compares to the total of your monthly expenses.

To complete the Monthly IES you will need a months' worth of pay stubs (or the knowledge of what your total monthly income is), a copy of all your monthly bills, and a good idea of how much your other expenses (such as groceries, clothing, and gas for your car) total every month.

Then, you take a regular sheet of lined notebook paper and all you need to do is draw a line, from top to bottom, down the middle of that sheet. What you now have on that sheet is two columns and one of those two columns you label with the heading "Income" and, the other, "Expenses."

Now, in the Income column you list each individual source of all your monthly income.

That might only be a single entry if you only get paid once a month, two entries if you get paid twice a month, or more than that if you get paid once a week or have some other sources of income other than your regular paychecks, alimony or child support, for example.

Then you add those all together to arrive at your total monthly income. Next, in the Expense column, you list…you guessed it—all your expenses! Easy, right?

If your income varies from month to month, you will need to determine your average monthly income.

If you cannot readily establish that, you will need to use estimates at this time and, then, write in the actual amounts as the year progresses. Remember, this is a document you fill out monthly.

At this point, you want to subtract the total of your bills and other expenses from your net income not your gross income.

Your *Net Income* is the money you actually see in your check, usually after the various taxes have already been deducted. The amount you see before those deductions is what is known as your Gross Income.

Monthly Net Income is what you actually have to spend or otherwise allocate every month (say, for example—save!). Money paid in taxes, although you earned it, is already accounted for by Uncle Sam and his relatives including Social Security (OASDI) and Medicare.

Also, if you have any recurring bills that you pay on some schedule other than monthly, you need to list those also. An example of a bill that is usually due on some schedule other than monthly might be your automobile insurance payment. Automobile insurance, for example, is usually billed every six or twelve months and not monthly.

This exact example might not apply in your case but it should give you an idea of the kind of expense I want you to consider. In order to determine your expenses in this regard, it might prove helpful to review your past credit card and checking account statements to look for these kinds of intermittent bills.

You will need to prorate every intermittent bill you do have to arrive at the amount to include on the appropriate line of your Monthly IES.

For example, let's say you have a bill for automobile insurance that comes due every six months and let's also assume that the amount of that bill is $600. All you do to prorate that amount is to take the amount of the bill ($600) and divide it by the number of months in the billing cycle (6).

$600 divided by 6 (months) is $100 and that is the amount you need to add to the total of your monthly bills on your Monthly Income and Expense Statement. If you fail to add these intermittent expenses to Monthly IES, your expense total will not be accurate.

Once you have entered all your monthly income on one side of the Monthly IES form and all your recurring monthly bills and expenses on the other, all you do is subtract the total of your monthly expenses from the total of your monthly income. The figure you arrive at when you do so is the total of your Monthly Discretionary Income, if any.

Your completed Monthly Income and Expense Statement will show you whether or not you are managing to spend less than you earn every month.

So, how are you doing in this regard?

If the number you end up with is positive, that is, if the total of your regular monthly bills and other expenses is less than what you earn, that is, obviously, a good thing. If, however, you are spending more than you earn, your financial situation is precarious, to say the least.

In fact, whether your bottom line is positive or negative at this point, the number you ended up with is almost certainly incorrect because a listing of your recurring spending does not capture all your actual costs of living. And, so, the number you arrive at this first time will most likely to be too low on the expense side of the ledger.

You will learn to refine your number, and get a truer picture of your financial condition, as you progress through the exercises in this book.

Chapter Twelve

Now, let's get back to the subject of worthless debt, and debt in general, and explore the subject in more depth.

The debt you owe is either secured or unsecured. The most common forms of secured debt are house and car loans. (A house loan is more properly referred to as a mortgage.)

If you are renting the place you live, the rent you pay is an expense as opposed to a debt but it is also somewhat "secured" in a way because if you don't pay the rent your landlord can boot you out.

Unsecured debt has nothing of value underlying the debt, itself. That is, there is no house to foreclose on or car to repossess if you fail to pay what you owe. And unsecured debt is both unsecured and the value of the debt is almost entirely consumed at the time of purchase— that's why I refer to worthless debt as consumer debt.

A good example of consumer debt is a restaurant meal paid for on a credit card. You are left with the debt but nothing to show for it. But, if you don't pay the bill when it comes due, it is not as if they can come to your house and take the meal back!

So, the only place unsecured consumer debt usually shows up, as I said, is on the liability side of your Net Worth Statement without any positive entry to offset it on the assets side of the ledger—it is, in fact, worse than worthless because it is actually dragging down the total of your Net Worth.

As an exercise, figure out exactly how much you are spending every month on debt repayment excluding your mortgage payment, if you have one. If you are like most people, that number might be as high as twenty percent of your gross income, or more, especially if you have a car loan. If you were to add in your mortgage, assuming you have one, that figure might just climb to fifty percent or more!

Are lenders crazy or something? I mean, how can they let people get in debt to the tune of fifty percent of their income and expect them to keep paying the bills?

In fact, it used to be that lenders were extremely wary of unsecured debt and understandably so. After all, a person could just walk away from such debt and leave the lender, holding the bag, so to speak.

It was this unsecured aspect of some lending that had to be addressed before the credit industry could become the financial juggernaut it is today.

The stroke of genius that made easy credit for unsecured debt a reality was the invention of the individual credit history. It made it much more consequential for a borrower to simply walk away from their debt because, if you did that, your ability to borrow in the future, for any debt whatsoever, secured or not, was severely impaired.

If you wreck your credit these days because you can't keep up with debt you owe on credit cards, it is likely to keep you from ever getting a home mortgage. And, too, many employers are now checking the credit history of job applicants to avoid hiring those who might be bringing external baggage to the job.

Individual credit histories were an absolute stroke of genius for the financial industry but, some might argue, not such a boon to individual consumers. Now, you can't just ignore a creditor's telephone call because they can take something from you of real value—your credit rating!

Most unsecured consumer debt is owed on credit cards of one sort or another although unsecured spending is sometimes financed with what is known as a signature loan. If you qualify, all you need to do to get a signature loan is sign the loan documents.

In other words, you do not need any other form of collateral to secure the loan other than your signature and, so, that is why it is called a signature loan. Signature loans, like credit cards, are a form of unsecured debt.

When someone is trapped in the cycle of growing consumer debt, the situation can feel hopeless but it is not hopeless. You have the power to turn it around and just being aware that you have that power should give you some hope. But it is a power that must be used correctly if you are to achieve the desired results.

When you find yourself in a situation that is causing you a problem, the first step to recovery is to face the facts and accept them for what they are. The next step is to formulate a plan to change the situation and begin to move in the desired direction.

Sometimes, though, people panic and do not sufficiently think out their response. When it comes to repaying debt, consumer credit card debt in particular, the initial reaction is usually the desire to want to pay it off as soon as possible.

When you react that way, however, you give up the power you have to exert control over the situation in a way that is more conducive to your own financial best interest.

Chapter Thirteen

Most of us understand at a sort of gut-level that consumer debt is not a good thing. Those of us living with a level of debt that we find troubling usually feel the urge to eliminate it as soon as possible. Unfortunately, rushing to pay off your debts will often serve to only make the situation worse.

Almost always, when someone is faced with an aggravating amount of consumer debt they attack the debt as if that was the problem—it is not! Debt is only the symptom of the actual problem. The real problem is what caused you to go in debt in the first place—your spending!

First, let's look at what happens when someone attacks the symptom rather than the problem. The likely scenario will go something like this: It is that time of the month when you sit down to pay the bills. Usually, this occurs right after you have received your latest paycheck so you're feeling a bit flush.

Your bills are laid out before you and those three or four (or more!) credit card bills irk you to no end. You have heard all the horror stories of how long it will take and how much it will cost in interest if you make only the minimum payment due, and so, in an effort to avoid that fate, you decide to send in a little extra.

But, when you are living paycheck to paycheck and particularly if you are spending more than you earn, it is almost always the case that even that little extra is too much and more than you can actually afford. So, when you do pay more than you can afford, what will usually happen then is you will run out of money before your next check arrives.

There is no such thing as extra money. Certainly, there was not any in your paycheck, so where did that extra you paid at the front-end come from? It can only come off the back-end, of course.

That extra you paid at the beginning of the month will leave you short at the end of the month and needing to cover the shortfall, again. What else can you do, since you have nothing left from your paycheck, except resort to charging that shortfall on a credit card?

Instead of making any real progress, when you pay more than you can afford, all you will have accomplished is made it almost certain that you will, once again, come up short at the end of the month. In other words, you have accomplished nothing!

When someone attempts to pay off their debt faster than they can afford to do so, a bad outcome is not only possible but likely. Our debts are the result of poor spending choices we made in the past but you can't do anything to change the past. But what you can do is change how you spend from now on, in the present, one day at a time.

Your focus, then, should be not on your debts but on your daily spending because it is the only place you can exercise any true measure of control. That is not to say that you will not take steps intended to get out of debt, you will, but those steps will not be the focus of your efforts.

It was your spending that created the debt in your life. And, as I explained, debt comes from living beyond your means and spending more than you earn. The first step, then, is to do what is necessary to stop the situation from getting worse by getting the total of your monthly spending below what you earn!

Part Three

Getting Zen

Chapter Fourteen

The first step to a more reasonable approach to settling your debts is to accept the fact that it will take about as long to get out of debt as it took you to get into it. After all, the chains of debt in which you now find yourself were cast one link at a time. And it is in that same way that the problem is best resolved.

If you are $5,000 in debt and it took you three years to get there, it will take you about three years to get out when you use a reasonable approach to debt repayment: Accept that and move on for it is the way to debt-free and prosperous living.

You will not get out of debt overnight but you can, over time. Do not try to rush the process at the expense of higher financial priorities. That rush-to-get-it-paid-off mentality is just a reflection of the desire for instant gratification that got you into this mess in the first place.

Don't let your debt exert any more power in your life than is already the case; calm down, remain calm and get a little Zen about it.

More and more, people are resorting to home equity lines of credit to pay off consumer debts. I think this trend will lead to more foreclosures than ever because it only addresses the symptom not the problem.

In fact, people are using home equity loans to enable consumer spending financed over ten, twenty, even thirty years! When you finance a debt like that, the results are low monthly payments but sooner or later the party has to end.

And, as soon as the money and the equity do run out, the spending frenzy will be forced to a screeching halt and the reality of their situation will be harsh. Sooner or later, we must all learn to live within our means. The longer you wait, the harder it will be to break the habit and more debt you will have run up.

Home equity loans do not address the root cause of debt and neither does bankruptcy. Certainly, both can feel like the solution but they have done nothing to address the real problem. Home equity lines of credit and bankruptcy are financial tools that do have their place, but when used to alleviate the ills of overspending, they are not the most prudent course. In fact, they are often mistakes, themselves.

It will help you to come to terms with your consumer debt if you accept your debts as simply the symptom of the actual issue which is spending.

Do not fall into the trap of giving up the power you have to settle your debts in a way that is most conducive to your own well-being. That power can be summed up in three simple words: Pay the minimum!

I know it sounds counter-intuitive somehow and, certainly, it goes against the more popular wisdom of the day but, the fact is, there are better ways to spend your money than repaying consumer debt. Certainly, it will need to be repaid, but that repayment should be made on a schedule that is most conducive to your financial well-being.

What I aim to teach you in this book is not just how to get out of debt but also how to stay out of debt—from now on and forever!

You won't make any real progress towards either of those goals by attacking a symptom of what is actually causing your debt. And, when you do pay the minimum, you will not only take control over your debts, you will be able to forget them, altogether!

Paying off your debts is not and should not be allowed to become your most important financial goal. There are many goals that should come before it. The dreams your goals represent and your future, for example.

Certain steps must absolutely take precedence over other steps in achieving greater financial security. That is important to remember because, the fact is, your financial resources are not unlimited. And your first financial priority is to build a certain amount of financial viability.

Remember, money you earn in the present goes either to support spending you have done in the past, the expenses you have today, or spending you plan to do in the future. In other words, your money has a lot of work to do. By paying the minimum, you will be addressing the issue of yesterday but with the least amount of negative impact on more important priorities.

In this way, you focus on what is truly important—your future—but without losing sight of concerns that still need to be addressed.

On the other hand, and in comparison, when you choose to pay more than the minimum on your debts, what you are telling yourself, in a very real sense, is that your debts are more important than both your dreams and your future.

Are they? Of course not! You only have so much money after all. So, what's it going to be—your debts or your dreams? But before you jump to any conclusions here, let me explain the plan in more detail.

Chapter Fifteen

My Pay-the-Minimum Plan actually has two phases to it. Phase One applies until you have that six-months' worth of expenses stashed in savings. Once you have that amount saved, you then transition to Pay-the-Minimum Phase Two.

The amount you pay during Phase One will be the actual total of the minimums required on all your variable credit debt.

For example, if you have three credit cards and the total of the minimum payments due is $100, that is how much you will pay that month—the minimum.

Next month, however, assuming no new charges, the total of the minimum payments due will be slightly lower. And, assuming the total of all your other expenses have remained the same, you will have more money to put away in savings.

Not much, I know, but when your financial security is shaky, every little bit helps. And, not only that, the total of your monthly expenses will also be that much lower.

Again, not much lower, I know, but, combined with other reductions you are able to make, your financial position is better than it was last month. And it will better still next month and the month after that and, if you stick to The Plan, from now on!

Once you have achieved your savings goal of having an amount equal to six months' worth of living expenses in the bank, it is time to move into Phase Two of the Pay-the-Minimum Plan.

In Phase Two the strategy changes a little. Whereas in Phase One you were paying less and less each month, now that you have achieved your savings goal your financial position is such that you afford to apply more towards paying off your debts—but not much more—because your money still has a lot of work to do!

In Phase Two you take whatever the total of all the "minimum" payments required is equal to in the first month after you have achieved your savings goal and freeze that as the monthly amount you will pay towards your debts, from that point forward, until they are completely paid off.

Let's say, for the sake of example, that you owe $5,000 in total consumer debt. It really doesn't matter to the process whether you owe this amount on one credit card or one dozen. What does matter, and the number you will need to know in order to implement Phase Two, is the total amount of all the minimum payments due at this point in time.

The card companies generally require a minimum payment of about four percent of the outstanding balance owed on the card. In this example, then, that would amount to $200. We will label the month in which you sent in that $200 payment as Phase Two/Month One.

If you were to pay that amount and not incur any new charges, the next month the minimum payment required would be slightly less than $200. But what you do is continue to send in the same amount as you did in Month One, a total of $200.

Now this next step in the process is very important:

When you pay one bill off, you take the money you were paying on that bill and add it to the payment amount of whichever remaining bill has the highest interest rate. When that bill is paid in full, you move on to the next using the same strategy until all your consumer debts are paid in full.

Once the plan is in place, you can then forget about these bills because they will eventually be paid off—but only if you stop adding to the total of your credit card debt. And, what that means, of course, is that you must stop spending (and charging!) more than you earn. Breaking the credit card habit is the only way you will ever settle your debts.

The plan to pay the minimum has a better chance of succeeding than does paying some larger amount for one very good reason—it leaves you more income.

And the more income you keep, the less likely you are to come up short at the end of the month. At first this might not be much but—hey!—twenty bucks less to a credit card bill means twenty bucks more in your pocket and that much less of a chance that you will be forced to credit card debt to make up the difference!

Remember, the first two goals of The Plan are, one, to help you bring your spending into alignment with what you earn, and, two, to help you build your savings. The third goal of The Plan is to not only to pay off your debts but to do so in a way that is most likely to help you achieve goals number one and two, as well.

But the aspect of The Plan that my clients find most compelling is that, once they get to Phase Two, they can pretty much forget about their debt, altogether! They know their debt is being addressed and they can move on with their lives.

One client told me that, once she got to Phase Two, it felt like a weight had been lifted off of her shoulders. She no longer had to wonder where the money to pay the bills would come from and her evenings at home were, at last, free from the dread of telephone calls from bill collectors.

Another success story from the archives of *The Debt Whisperer*!

Chapter Sixteen

Once you have committed to pay the minimum and have put The Plan in action, the next step will be to focus on the actual cause of that debt—overspending.

First, let me reiterate our working definition of overspending: Overspending is spending more in any one month than you earned in that month.

Spending is best managed on a month to month basis because it is provides a timeframe to your budgeting that most of us can most readily relate to. The goal, then, is to reduce your spending on that same monthly basis and to not incur any new debt.

As simple as that goal might sound, however, it is not, necessarily easy. In fact, it can prove very difficult to rein in your spending once you are trapped in that cycle of overspending and growing debt.

The trick to getting your monthly spending under the total of your monthly income is to comb your present day expenses and expenditures with an eye towards reducing where you can to create some immediate space in your budget. It is that space that will allow you to put your credit cards away.

Any reductions you can make in your budget will help, of course, but you should aim to reduce your monthly spending by a percentage equal to the total of your consumer debt divided by your total annual income.

For example, let's say you owe a total of $4,000 in consumer debt and that your annual income is $40,000. $4,000 divided by $40,000 equals ten percent (4,000/40,000 = 0.1) and that would be the ideal amount by which to aim to cut your monthly spending.

Why? Because that percentage figure is likely to be the same amount by which, on average, you are overspending every month. Your actual figure might be higher or lower than that in the example but, in order to reduce your monthly budget at all, you will need to have a monthly budget in the first place.

If you are in debt and you do not use a budget to manage your spending, that is part of your problem and part of the solution. If you already use a budget and you have still gotten into debt, then your budget does not accurately reflect what you are actually spending—more on that later.

Depending on your particular situation, severe measures might even be required but, as severe as they might feel to you, you should remember that any inconvenience or discomfort they might cause you is likely to be short-lived.

These are steps taken to right your ship and they do not necessarily have to represent long-term lifestyle adjustments.

You see, even if the amount by which you are overspending from month to month is not a lot, the months add up quickly and small amounts can add up to a substantial sum almost before you realize what is happening. Then, even if do manage to keep the wolves at bay, your growing debt will become the cause of more and more stress and less and less financial security.

So, how do we respond to the stress of all these bills piling up? Well, if you listen to the pundits and what passes for good advice these days, you send in extra money you really don't have just to feel as if you are doing something about the problem. But there is no such thing as extra money—all your money has a job to do!

And, when you do send in that extra (not really extra!) money, what will usually happen next is that the last paycheck will run out before the next paycheck comes in.

And it is in that gap where we are forced to resort to credit. What you need to do is close that gap by paying the minimum and cutting expenses. It is possible to step off the debt treadmill and the way to do that is by finding whatever room you can in your present spending to give yourself some breathing room.

Hold a garage sale, stop eating at restaurants, join a carpool, turn off cable TV service; drastic times call for drastic measures but, remember, it is not forever it is, at worst, a temporary inconvenience.

And, really, in the grander scheme of things, it's your financial security and peace of mind that are at stake. The measures mentioned, after all, represent a choice you make to achieve a more positive outcome not a sacrifice.

A sacrifice is when parents choose to go without eating so that their children will have enough. It is not a sacrifice when you choose to forego dinner out and keep those thirty or forty dollars in your pocket and off your credit card balance. (Although I know it can feel like you are being unbearably tough on yourself!)

Later on, when your financial position is stronger, it is likely that you will have the money to add some of the cuts you made back into your budget, *if* you choose to do so. But the chances are that, after you have lived without something for a while, you might just decide you didn't need it, after all!

Chapter Seventeen

Earlier, I mentioned the process of combing through your expenditures to look for spending to cut from your budget. This is an absolutely critical exercise and what you want to accomplish, through the process of closely examining your spending, is to make it less likely that you will need to resort to debt to artificially increase your income.

It is generally accepted that there are two types of spending, discretionary and non-discretionary. Those expenses or debt payments that we are absolutely obligated to pay represent non-discretionary spending. This includes expenditures such as court-mandated payments, child-support payments, for example.

Some people put expenditures such as rent, the mortgage payment, and utilities in the non-discretionary category but I do not think they absolutely belong there.

Some part of the spending we do on food can, certainly, be defined as non-discretionary. I mean, we all need to eat. But at least some of the food most of us buy we could just as easily do without and, so, it actually represents discretionary spending.

Discretionary spending is any spending you can just say no to—the CD or DVD you can live without, that new pair of shoes to go with the other twenty pairs you already have sitting in your closet, or adding dessert to your restaurant tab when you are already stuffed, anyway!

And, whether it is a variable expense like groceries or gas for your car, or a debt with the same fixed amount due every month like your mortgage or a car payment, what you want to do is reduce or eliminate some of your discretionary spending in order to create a margin between what you earn and what you spend.

Let me give you a tip—all of your spending is discretionary. Accepting that statement as a fact is a big mental step towards changing the belief system that has led to many of our money problems. Even court-mandated payments are subject to review if your financial situation is dire enough to truly (truly) warrant it.

Rent, food, utilities, car payments, even the mortgage are all subject to being considered for being cut to create some immediate space between what you earn and what you spend.

And, depending on just how deep you are willing to cut, changing the course of your financial life might well result in taking some drastic measures.

These measures could include selling your house and moving into a rental, finding a roommate to share living expenses, selling a car on which you have a loan and using the proceeds to buy a car for which you can pay cash—heck, it might even mean selling the car and taking the bus for a while!

The extent to which you are willing to go depends entirely on how quickly you want to enhance your level of financial security by increasing your savings.

The process includes facing up to and accepting the life you can actually afford to live based on your present income. This does not mean you will be locked into this life forever. Your income will increase and as you settle your debts you will free up more money to fund lifestyle enhancements.

But, remember, it is very likely that many of the material goods on which you are presently spending your money are robbing you of your potential not enhancing the likelihood of your achieving it! No, not every dollar you spend will find its way to your bottom line but that should at least be a consideration in the transaction because it is that consideration that will help you measure the true cost of every purchase you make.

And, when I say true cost, I mean the cost in terms of the negative effect your spending is having on your peace of mind, financial and otherwise.

Peace of mind is a zero-sum equation; all aspects of your life add or subtract from your bottom line in that regard. If your worries are keeping you awake at night it doesn't matter what the exact cause of those worries are, you are awake, nevertheless.

The shovel that most people use to dig their financial hole is credit cards. If that applies to you, let me say this, again—you can't make any real progress until you break the charge card habit. That is the fundamental rule of eliminating debt from your life.

To do that, to break your dependence on credit to supplement your income, you need to make the commitment that you will spend what you earn but absolutely no more as you begin to implement the Pay-the-Minimum Plan.

Once you are clear on that, you then begin the process of being really conscious of every dollar you spend. This is an on-going process of examining every item in your budget and every dollar you spend at the moment the transaction is about to take place with an eye towards reducing, deferring, or eliminating wherever and whenever possible in order to spend less of what you earn.

Chapter Eighteen

A big step in controlling your spending will be to get back in touch with your spending. And the way you begin to do *that* is to pay cash when you shop: Leave your credit cards at home and spend using only cash—not checks, not debit cards—cash!

The main reason to spend using cash is that various surveys have revealed that we tend to spend somewhere between ten and thirty percent **more** when we pay using some means other than cash. And the difference is greatest when we shop with a credit card!

At some intuitive level, you can probably understand this phenomenon. When you pay with plastic, it doesn't quite feel as real as when you count out your hard-earned dollars.

A lot of the spending that many of us do is done at a sort of emotional distance—just whip out the plastic, no big deal, it's not real money, anyway—and without much attention to the what is going on or the impact of the transaction on our finances.

In order to reduce your spending, however, you will need to be very much "in the moment" at the moment that money is changing hands or you are deciding whether to add another doo-dad to your shopping basket.

You see, that is the decision point at which you can still exert some control and when you need to ask yourself: Is this money well spent? In other words, you need to stay closely connected to the act—be here now!

When you spend using a credit card, or even a check or debit card, you are taking just the opposite approach—you are distancing yourself from the transaction and it is that distance that makes it much easier to spend more than you had planned to and, even, more than you can afford to.

I mean, after all, credit cards and debit cards and checking accounts were all invented to make it easier for you to spend. It should not be your goal to make spending as easy as possible.

Yes, if you are going to pay with cash, you will need to plan your shopping more carefully—but that is a good thing! Yes, you will need to leave the house with enough cash to cover what you plan to buy but, again, that will keep you from spending more than you had planned to spend.

And, if you only have enough cash for those items on your shopping list, you won't have enough for any impulsive buying.

No one needs more than one or, at the most, two credit cards. If you have more than that, now is the time to consider closing some of those accounts as it is in no way helpful to carry a bunch of credit cards around with you when you shop.

If you are presently counting on the credit limit on those excess cards to fall back on in case of a financial emergency, you should at least leave them at home.

Or, better yet, keep them secured in a safety deposit box at your bank or other financial institute. That way they will not be so readily available. Then, as the balance in your savings account permits, you can cancel those excess cards.

And, yes, I know that closing an account can sometimes have a slightly negative effect on your credit score. But that is a small price to pay for the benefit of removing yourself from harm's way (in the form of the temptation of another credit card). That benefit far outweighs the short-term hit to your credit.

Chapter Nineteen

There is a repayment hierarchy into which your consumer debts can be placed. The higher the interest rate you are paying on any individual debt, the higher in the repayment hierarchy it should be ranked.

Another factor to consider in ranking a debt for payoff is the effect it has on the bottom line of your Net Worth Statement.

Unsecured consumer debt, for example, will almost always drag the amount of your Net Worth down. This is because the debt is entered on the liability side of your Net Worth Statement but there is no entry to offset it, even partially, on the asset side of the ledger.

Paying off this kind of worthless, unsecured debt should be a priority but the effect of some secured debts on your Net Worth can be just as negative. Vehicles are a prime example of this. Let's now explore this issue in more depth as it is an important concept:

For many of us, the equity in our homes represents a large portion of our Net Worth. And this makes sense because, for most of us, our home is almost always the largest single purchase we will ever make.

If you are buying your home, the outstanding balance of the mortgage on it represents a liability but its market value represents an asset entry on the positive side of your Net Worth Statement. Vehicles on which we carry a loan will also impact both sides of our Net Worth Statement in that same way.

When you purchase a vehicle, a new vehicle in particular, the effect on your Net Worth will almost always be negative—sometimes disastrously so! And, if you finance the purchase using an auto loan, you can sometimes end up being "upside down" in that loan. You are upside down in a loan when you owe more on the vehicle than it would be likely to sell for.

You have probably heard the term, "house-rich but cash-poor." It is usually used to refer to someone whose house payment leaves them with little slack in their budget and is meant to imply that someone has over-extended in order to finance their home.

It is my experience, however, that more people today are car-rich but cash-poor than ever before, having committed to financing vehicles that are draining their resources away from funding more important financial needs.

And a person will voluntarily put his or herself into this position and gladly take the financial hit just to be able to drive a vehicle they really can't afford and could just as easily do without! House-rich and car-rich might seem to be the same sort of financial condition but only until you take a look at the impact that each has on your bottom line.

A $25,000 car will lose something like twenty percent of its value the minute you drive it off the dealer's lot. That amounts to an instant loss of $5,000 that gets subtracted right off the bottom line of your Net Worth Statement.

And the impact on your Net Worth will usually get even worse from that point! If you have a five-year loan on a vehicle, it is likely that the negative impact to your Net Worth at the end of year one will be as high as thirty percent or more of the original purchase price.

And all the payments you have been making are nowhere to be seen—they have only served to limit the total of the negative impact!

It is a very different picture when you look at the affect that being house-poor will have on your Net Worth. If your home has a present-day value of $200,000 and is appreciating five percent a year, that $10,000 in appreciation in the coming year will add to and grow your Net Worth.

And—check this out—the amount of that appreciation is compounded one year to the next if the market continues to rise! Compounded appreciation is the only financial force more powerful than compounded interest!

Also, the mortgage payments you make serve to pay down the principal amount of the mortgage and add even more to the total of your assets. So, as you can see, there is a very big difference between being house-poor and being car-poor.

Meanwhile, the auto industry is doing all they can to make it as easy as possible for you to fall into their trap. The auto industry offers all sorts of smoke and mirror financing and sales incentives to move their products; giving with one hand while taking away with the other. It's the oldest con in the world!

Zero-interest loans are just one more version of this slight-of-hand. Those who fall victim to zero-interest financing often pay top-dollar for their vehicle, losing any benefit of the seemingly favorable financing terms.

When you factor in all the other costs of driving and the fact that most families own two vehicles or more, transportation costs can literally go through the roof and end up costing you much more than what you pay for your home over a lifetime of buying and driving vehicles.

The Automobile Association of America estimated that the average total cost to operate a private vehicle in 2003 was fifty-six cents per mile. This includes vehicle acquisition costs and operating costs such as fuel and insurance.

If you drive just 15,000 miles a year and drive for 50 years, the two car total comes to 1,500,000 miles and at a cost of $840,000! If you could you cut that figure in half, you could add as much as $500,000 to your Net Worth by the time you retire.

Now, if you are in your twenties or thirties, retirement might seem like nothing more than a vague concept to you. Meanwhile, in the here and now, the thought of driving a shiny new car is much more appealing than saving money for some distant dream.

But, by following just three simple rules, you will save a substantial amount of money in this area of your finances; and those three rules are to buy used, never finance for more than three years, and keep every vehicle for at least five years after you pay off the loan.

These rules, however, as simple as they are, can be a real test of your self-discipline when it comes to facing up to the constant bombardment of the auto industry as they push their wares. They spend millions of dollars every year to spread the gospel of the SUV and Hummer!

And where does the money come from to pay for all that advertising? Well, if you buy what they're selling, some part of it will come right out of your pocket.

I fell for their siren-song when I was younger; it is a mistake many of us make. The good news is that the day you change your buying habits is the day your recovery will begin.

Having a car is a practical accommodation to the realities of modern life; the trick to money well spent is to get where you're going while, at the same time, making room in your budget to build real financial security.

Chapter Twenty

Now, there are some financial pundits who would advise you to save and pay cash every time you purchase a vehicle. But I don't believe that is the best financial move unless and until all your other financial goals have been achieved. And, even then, you should carefully weigh your other options.

Yes, you will pay interest on a car loan, but when you pay cash you will lose the interest that money could have been earning if you had not spent it on the vehicle. When you spend money on one thing, you lose the opportunity to spend it somewhere else—that is what is known as "opportunity cost."

And, when you spend money, you also lose the opportunity to save that money, instead. This is important, so let me explain this statement in more detail (and in bold type to make sure you get the point!):

No money is more expensive than the money you spend today because it stops the power of compounded interest.

No less a mind than Albert Einstein called compound interest the eighth wonder of the world and the greatest mathematical discovery of all time! Pretty strong words for the guy who put together E=MC2, wouldn't you say?

Nothing will enhance your financial security, perceived and actual, quite like money in the bank. But, when you choose to spend when you could have saved, you also surrender that same amount of ready-cash liquidity, which you will wish you had if the need ever arises.

If it is time for you to make a vehicle purchase, I recommend you consider a mid-range, low-mileage used car that is in good condition and at least three years old. A car like that will save you as much as fifty percent of its original purchase price and cost somewhere between eight and twelve thousand dollars.

Certainly, that figure represents a substantial savings but it is still a lot of money! And I don't believe it is the best financial decision you can make to choose to have that amount of cash tied up in a depreciating asset.

And it is a really bad idea if you have any unsecured debt or don't have an amount of savings equal to six months' worth of living expenses.

In fact, I would rather see it drawing interest in a CD even if all your other financial ducks are in a row and even if you are paying more in interest on the loan than you are earning on the money in the bank. Why? Well, a couple of reasons.

One, the money will always be there in case you need it and, two, the money will always be there in case you need it! Hello!

When, instead, you sink ready-cash into a vehicle purchase and you suddenly need the money, you might be forced to sell the car and to somehow do without. Not only that but, in that situation, you might even have to sell the car for less than it is actually worth in order to cash out as quickly as possible!

If you don't have the money in your budget to support a loan payment but you do have the money to pay cash, you might consider depositing the money in an accessible, long-term, interest-bearing account like a money-market account, for example, and making the payment from the balance of that account.

By doing so, you reduce the total amount of interest you pay while still maintaining the maximum amount of cash liquidity and financial security.

Sure, you're going to pay some interest on the loan but it will be worth it to maintain a more positive financial position. And, if you shop smart for both the vehicle and the loan, the difference between the interest the money earns and what you are paying can be kept to a minimum.

A final consideration in weighing your financial options when it comes to paying cash or financing a vehicle purchase is, what I call, the endowment factor.

In working with my clients, I have found that few of them are familiar with the concept of an "endowment." Just in case it is new to you, as well, I will explain the concept a bit more in the following chapter.

Chapter Twenty-One

Most major universities and many large charitable foundations finance some portion of their operations using proceeds from, what is known as, an "endowment."

An endowment, for our purposes, can be thought of as a sort of special type of savings account. The amount of an endowment for a major university, for example, can run into the billions of dollars and it will earn millions of dollars of interest—year after year! And it is the interest from that endowment that the university will use, in part, to fund operations.

But what is important for you to know is that any institution that does use the interest proceeds from an endowment to finance their operations will avoid ever spending any of the principal of that endowment. Why? Because spending the capital portion of the endowment will forever lower the amount of interest it will earn.

In fact, they always plan to spend less every year than the total amount of the interest they expect to earn in that year because, by doing so, the size of the endowment will continue to grow.

The financial-types who earn a living managing large endowments are among the sharpest tools in the shed, so pay attention to how they manage that money. And you should follow their example to the extent that you consider your savings as your "personal endowment" and never spend the principal.

There is a story told about a man who is shunned by everyone in his ultra-conservative community. When an outsider asks one of the locals why, he is told, simply, "he dipped into his capital."

Money is hard to come by and, while spending your savings should not make you a pariah in your community, you should always be reluctant to let go of it too easily or when it is not absolutely necessary that you do so.

That is not to imply that you should be miserly but, rather, that you spend smartly. You can probably find better uses for your money than locking up big chunks of it in a depreciating asset, such as a vehicle.

Financial independence is achieved by replacing income from work with income from interest on savings (not investments because you can't count on the return from investments in the short-term).

It will be your personal endowment, that is, the total amount you have saved and that is earning you interest, that will provide you with some, if not all, of the income you will need to achieve financial independence and kiss the rat race goodbye someday.

The sooner you get money into your endowment and growing, the better. So, instead of paying cash for a vehicle, make a down payment that will be just enough to make the payments on a three-year loan fit well within your budget and put the rest to work—forever—in a personal endowment of your own.

That is how the great universities do it, that is how the wealthy do it, and that is how you should do it too!

In the following section of the book you will learn a way to manage your income that will make you virtually debt-proof.

Part Four

The Road to Dream Street

Chapter Twenty-Two

A major cause of debt and financial upset is the failure to account for all of our actual costs of living. Even if we manage our finances using a budget, some of our expenses simply escape us and, so, go unaccounted for until they actually come due.

When you let that happen, that is, when you fail to account for all your expenses in your Monthly Budget, the effects of doing so can cascade through your entire financial life. The problem is that not all of your expenses are all that easy to deal with unless and until you learn how to do so.

A few years ago, I suffered my own financial setback and as part of my recovery I began using a budget for the first time in my life. What I soon learned is that learning to use a budget effectively was like learning any other skill—it takes time.

One of the issues I encountered was how to account for bills and other expenses that came due on some schedule other than monthly. Earlier in this book I showed you how to deal with intermittent expenses like that.

The other problem I had when I was learning to budget was how to plan for expenses that seemed to pop up sort of unexpected-like. I say unexpected-like because they weren't exactly out-of-the-blue but they always seemed to catch me unprepared.

For example, I knew I would probably have a dental emergency of some sort once or twice a year but, then again, maybe not if I got lucky.

How do you budget for something like that? Well, I finally figured it out after a few dead-ends and false starts. And, later, when I taught personal financial management at the college level, I learned that others were facing the same issues.

Also, in my work as a Personal Money Coach, I saw my clients struggle with budgeting that was well-intentioned but often off the mark. In time, after careful consideration of the issue and reviewing the budget issues that came up with my clients, I discovered why their budgets were failing.

The problem was that the budgets that weren't working were not, in fact, all inclusive. In other words, they were missing regularly recurring expenses.

When you leave an expense (or expenses!) out of your budget, a budget cannot be the tool it is intended to be because the numbers will be wrong. And, so, all the planning you do and all the assumptions you make based on those numbers will, likewise, also be wrong.

"What's going on here?" I wondered. My clients were working hard to get this right and, yet, their monthly budgets were off, sometimes by hundreds of dollars. The problem, I learned over time, is that we do not get billed for some of our regular recurring expenses. Let me explain:

One cost that often goes unconsidered in our monthly budgeting is the fact that everyday every *thing* we own is wearing out to one extent or another and will, eventually, need to be replaced if it is something we can't live without.

Take, for example, the tires on your vehicle: Every time you drive your car, the tires experience some wear and that wear is adding up. Now, you can choose to ignore that wear but eventually, it is a bill that will come due. And, when it does, the question then is: will you be ready for it?

I have often been asked how to budget for unexpected expenses. Most often, my response is that there are very few expenses that are actually unexpected. Certainly, tires wearing out and the fact that they will someday need to be replaced can hardly be defined as unexpected. That is what tires do—they wear out!

Likewise, the clock on every appliance you own is ticking because you know that not one of them will last forever. The same thing is also happening to the car you drive—it's wearing out.

And clothes are also wearing out and shoes are wearing down. The TV could go any day and who knows when a tooth will begin to ache! Time and use both take a toll and that toll is a bill that will eventually come due.

So none of the examples mentioned fall into the category of an unexpected expense. But they are costs that are difficult to account for until you know how to do so.

These kinds of expenses are also are easy to overlook (or, even ignore) and, so, are often not adequately planned for in our Monthly Budget. The only way to actually address these kinds of expenses is, first, to identify them all and, second, to include a line item in your Monthly Budget to build up a fund adequate to pay the bill when it comes due.

We all know that expenses like these are bound to happen, even if it is not entirely possible to know when, exactly, they will arrive. But ignoring these expenses by failing to adequately plan for them is a major reason why budgets fail.

Unexpected expenses are not really unexpected. Unexpected expenses are really expenses for which we fail to plan and they can often be that proverbial last straw that can break our financial back because, when an unplanned for expense does comes along, we have only a few options for coming up with the money we need—none of which are conducive to our financial peace of mind.

One option you have when a bill like this pops up is to simply not pay it. This might even be a viable option if it is something you can live without.

Another option will be to find the money you need from somewhere else in your budget. Unfortunately, doing that will almost certainly result in some other bill (or bills!) going unpaid.

When you exercise this option, you can end up juggling bills and trying to play catch up for months and months! The name given to this second option is "robbing Peter to pay Paul" and, although it is an option, it is almost never a good idea.

And, finally, the third option that might be available is to pay the expense by charging it to a credit card—in effect, being forced to borrow the money in order to meet an expense for which we failed to plan.

This is probably the most popular option and it is the way most of us deal with the issue when it comes up—time after time. But as popular as it is, it is not the way this issue should actually be addressed.

This, then, is how our, so-called, money troubles usually begin. An expense that goes unplanned for is like the first domino in a long line that, once it is tipped, goes on to take down all the others. Borrowing is often the first step to a financial meltdown and it can be the beginning of the end because borrowed money will always, eventually, need to be repaid.

Chapter Twenty-Three

First of all, let's call borrowed money by its real name—credit! And what credit usually translates to in the real world is charging the bill to one credit card or another. But, when you use credit to compensate for inadequate planning, it can often be the start of mounting credit card debt.

But when you add to the already existing total of your debt load to cover budget shortfalls, the result will be that the total of your credit card debt will go up and with it the monthly amount of the minimum payment due.

Then, when the bill comes due, the additional money to pay the higher bill will need to come from somewhere else in your budget. It is finding that money that can be the problem, particularly if you are already overspending or living paycheck to paycheck.

But wait, you say, what about my savings?

Well, the truth is, that is exactly where most of us will turn if that is an option. But when you do that, it is a clear signal that your Monthly Budget is not accurate. And, so, money you thought you were saving turns out to be nothing more than bad accounting!

And, then, when the next unplanned for expense comes along, whether it's a toothache that is going to need a root canal and crown or the tires that give up the ghost, a tight budget can get even tighter. You can see where this can lead over time, right?

Usually, it will lead right back to the plastic and yet more debt. And, then, it's yet another bill or a higher amount to accommodate in your already tight budget. It is a vicious and self-perpetuating cycle. Your peace of mind can't help but be affected in a negative way when you are always living in dread of the next financial surprise you just know is coming!

The good news is that you can, in fact, plan for these kinds of expenses. They don't have to take you by surprise or find you unprepared. You can manage your finances so that you are, in fact, prepared to meet these expenses each and every time they come due, even if you don't know exactly when that will be.

Chapter Twenty-Four

In order for a Monthly Budget to be the tool it is intended to be, it must actually include all of your monthly expenses. When you do not identify all your expenses, you are almost certain to overspend and some or all of the money you think you are saving will be, in fact, an illusion.

The fact is that most of us underestimate our actual cost of living. Let's reconsider that tire example I used in the last chapter: Every mile you drive is depreciating the asset your tires represent but how many of us prorate the cost of new tires on a monthly basis?

And, as I mentioned before, the clock is ticking on every appliance you own. For example, let's consider your washing machine (if you don't have one, work with me here!). You can expect that a washing machine will last about ten years or so but, unless you budget for its replacement over its useful life, you will be financially unprepared when it dies and the dirty clothes are piling up.

But those sorts of costs are only one example of expenses that often get overlooked and go unaccounted for in an otherwise well-intentioned budget. And, as I mentioned, those intermittent bills that come due on some schedule other than monthly are also the cause of a lot of unnecessary financial distress.

Certainly, you could meet these unplanned for expenses with money from your savings but, then, that money is not really savings, is it?

All of the recurring and actual costs associated with your lifestyle must be accounted for in your Monthly Budget.

Instead of dipping into your savings or resorting to more credit card debt to compensate for a lack of planning, better planning is what is actually required to address this issue.

And, those costs and expenses that don't fit neatly into a Monthly Budget format are, in fact, readily addressed using, what I call, a Reserve Account.

I call them "Reserve Accounts" because that is what they are—money put aside and held in reserve for expenses that you know are bound to arrive someday, even if we don't know exactly when the bill will come due.

A Reserve Account is also handy tools that you can use to manage other aspects of your spending, as well, but their primary purpose is to act as a place-holder in your Monthly Budget.

The first thing you need to do is identify those costs that you have overlooked in the past and that are presently going unaccounted for in your budget. I have already mentioned a couple, tires and medical bills, but those are just two examples but there many others. I recommend that you dig through your financial records for the last two years or so in order to ferret them out.

An easy way to begin the process of identifying these expenses will be to review a years' worth of checking and charge card statements.

For example, take medical expenses not covered by health insurance. If a review of your records shows that over the last twelve months you spent $600 in this category, you simply divide that number by twelve to arrive at the prorated, monthly cost of this expense, $50.

Once you have identified each of the expenses that you want to manage using a Reserve Account, you add the monthly amount of each of them and that is the amount that you would plug into your Monthly Budget as "Reserve Total."

That Reserve Total line item would be an amount equal to the total of all your Reserve Accounts, so, you do not need to account for each Reserve Account individually in your Monthly Budget unless it is something you want to do.

Now, you need a place to keep the money in all your Reserve Accounts. Your regular checking account won't work and neither will your savings account. If you put your Reserve Account funds into either of those accounts, it is too hard to keep them separate and that money is likely to be spent, whether intentionally or not.

The answer, then, is to open a second checking account just for your Reserve Account deposits, what I call your Reserve Checking Account and that is where you deposit the $50 you're putting away every month to meet medical expenses.

With your Reserve Account in place and the money in your Reserve Checking Account, when an expense pops up you won't need to rob Peter to pay Paul or resort to charging it on a credit card.

Now, all you do is write a check for it out of your Reserve Checking Account. And, when all of your costs are accounted for in this way, you will be debt-proof. And you will have largely eliminated the element of surprise from your financial life.

Reserve Accounts are like instant karma or something! Before Reserve Accounts you would probably curse your luck when the battery in your car died. Now, with money in the bank (in a Reserve Account for "Miscellaneous Auto Expenses"), it is no big deal—all you do is write the check and forget about it!

Nothing will change your financial luck for the better like better accounting!

The obvious problem with using Reserve Accounts is that it takes money to fund them. And that money will be hard to come by if your budget is already tight. But the fact is that funding these accounts is not an option.

I mean, think about it—if you don't have the money to save every month to replace your tires when they wear out, where will the money come from when the bill comes due?

It reminds me of a line from a commercial—you can pay me now or you can pay me later! And we all know that the "pay-me-later" road leads, almost always, to debt and stress.

Working with Reserve Accounts does take some practice. And it is likely to take you some time to find the money to fund all of the Reserve Accounts for which you identify a need.

So, when you begin working with Reserve Accounts, I recommend that you identify those two or three bills or expenses that always seem to catch you unprepared and set up a Reserve Account to fund each of them.

For example, car insurance is a common example of an expense we all have but for which we are billed only once or twice a year. So, how would you account for that in a Monthly Budget? Well, let's review the process one more time:

All you do is divide the total of the annual amount by twelve to arrive at the monthly amount and that is the amount you would deposit every month to your Reserve Account to pay the bill when it comes due.

Think about that for a minute and think about what is happening in one situation compared to the other.

In the typical, caught unprepared scenario, you are scrambling for the money and frustrated with your own lack of financial planning. While, on the other hand, when you have budgeted to pay the bill whenever it comes due, the money will be there waiting in your Reserve Account. Is that cool or what?

Right now, while you are thinking about this subject, use the lines below to list those expenses that are silently accumulating and that will eventually come due.

Remember some of the specific examples I have already mentioned such as tires for your vehicle, visits to the dentists, and appliances.

_____

_____

_____

_____

_____

Chapter Twenty-Five

Reserve Accounts are also a great tool for budgeting that spending that does need to be controlled or otherwise managed but does not otherwise fit readily into your Monthly Budget. Take the money you spend on gifts, for example.

Most of us just buy gifts using whatever money we have available. The money spent on gifts can really add up though, especially if we are not keeping track of the total and, even then, if we are spending without some sort of a self-imposed limit.

We actually have quite a few spending categories where this same sort of control would help us to better manage our spending; clothes being another example that most of us are familiar with. But, unless we have established a monthly allowance for these items in our budget, it is too easy to spend more than we intended and even more than we can actually afford.

A Reserve Account can help you to avoid both of those spending traps.

For example, let's say you want (or can afford) to spend no more than $1,200 a year on buying new clothes. That works out to $100 a month and this is the amount you would deposit each month to the Reserve Account named—guess what?—Clothes!

You will need to keep track of the balance in each individual Reserve Account on a monthly basis but you don't need a separate checking account for each of them.

Instead, you will deposit the monthly total of all your individual Reserve Accounts into a single checking account, your Reserve Checking Account, and you will pay any Reserve Account expense with money from that account.

For example, let's say you start with three Reserve Accounts and that each is funded every month with the following amounts:

Account Item	Amount of Monthly Funding
Car Insurance	$50
Auto Expenses	$25
Gifts	$35

That means that, every month, you would deposit the total of these amounts, $110, to your Reserve Checking Account.

You can keep track of the total amount of your Reserve Checking Account using the checkbook register you will get when you open that account but you will also need to account for the balance in each of your individual Reserve Accounts. The way you do that is by keeping an individual register for each of them.

Those individual registers work just like a checkbook register, that is, you enter your beginning balance, add deposits, and subtract withdrawals. Here is an example of what the register for the Reserve Checking Account would look like using the numbers from the previous example:

Date	Details	With.	Deposit	Balance
3/1	Monthly Funding		$110	$400
4/1	Monthly Funding		$110	$510
4/3	Auto Expenses	$75		$435
5/1	Monthly Funding		$110	$545
5/13	Gift	$45		$500

As you can see, each time a payment is made, you would include the name of the Reserve Account from which the withdrawal for that payment was made.

In the individual Reserve Account register, you would then enter the same financial information and a more detailed description of the transaction, itself for your reference.

I keep the register for each of my Reserve Accounts on an individual sheet of lined notebook paper. Each of those sheets I keep in a three-ring binder. I never have bothered to computerize the process even though I'm usually keeping around six or seven individual Reserve Accounts at any one time.

My point here, however, is simply this: How you do it is not as important as doing it!

Like learning to manage your finances using a Monthly Budget, you will get better at working with Reserve Accounts over time. Also, it is quite possible that an expense will come up for which the balance of the individual Reserve Account is insufficient. This is most likely to occur when you first begin funding an account.

The easiest (but most costly) way to avoid this from happening is to fund an account with three or four months of funding up front, although, I know this will not always be an option. If you have sufficient savings, you might consider using that money to "front-load" one or more Reserve Accounts.

By front-load, what I mean is that you determine the amount of monthly funding it will take to meet the bill when it comes due and, then, open the account with three or four times that amount or whatever it will take to get you "on schedule."

For example, if you insurance bill is coming due in four months and the amount due will be $432 but the prorated amount of your annual bill is only $72 a month, you would need to front-load the account with $144 to have enough when that bill comes due.

Chapter Twenty-Six

After a few months of funding your Reserve Accounts, the balance will begin to grow and could become quite substantial over time. Some accounts, those in which you incur few or, even, no expenses for a number of months can grow to an amount larger than is likely to ever be needed.

This is what happened in my Reserve Account for medical expenses. I went through a couple of years without any major medical expenses and the account grew to exceed the amount of what is called the annual catastrophic limit of my health insurance policy. That limit is the amount at which I no longer have to pay any deductible for covered services.

Once I had that amount in the account, I no longer needed to contribute any more to it. However, I did not quit making my monthly deposit entirely.

Instead, what I did was lower the amount of the monthly funding and, at the end of every year, I use any amount over the necessary balance to fund a negative balance in some other account or, simply, add it to savings.

If you do find yourself with an account that has a large annual surplus, it could mean that you should consider lowering the amount of your monthly contribution.

You never want to eliminate a Reserve Account as long as it is an expense that needs to be accounted for but you might consider combining some smaller individual expenses into a single account. I have a Reserve Account I use this way and it helps to reduce the number of individual accounts I need to keep track of.

Here, then, is where a very interesting aspect of Reserve Account funding can come into play:

In continuing with the previous example, let's say you have a couple of months of funding your four Reserve Accounts (car insurance, car expenses, gifts, and, now, clothes) under your belt and the total in those accounts and in your Reserve Checking Account is $420.

Now, let's say, you find a suit on sale for $300 but the register for your clothes account shows the balance to be only $200.

What can you do? You can actually borrow from the $420 total balance and buy the suit anyway, as long as you realize that any further clothes purchases will need to be curtailed until the other accounts are paid back.

The ability to borrow between Reserve Accounts is one of their most appealing features but, as attractive as it is, it must be used with great care and planning to avoid bad timing. When you borrow from one account or accounts for another, you need to be sure it won't leave you short for a bill that you know is coming due.

If your borrowing leaves you with $120 remaining in your Reserve Checking Account and next month's funding brings the total to $330 but you have a $350 automobile insurance payment due that month, you have over-borrowed. That is why I pointed out earlier that getting good at working with Reserve Accounts will take some time and practice. This is particularly the case when it comes to borrowing between accounts.

It will also help to avoid over-borrowing if you keep a calendar that shows when Reserve Account bills are coming due and that, when you do borrow, you keep that schedule in mind. Of course, this only applies to those bills that actually have a due date. It is not always prudent to borrow from those Reserve Accounts for expenses that happen when they happen, like a dental emergency.

Also, you can actually plan to borrow and not pay the borrowed amount back if you think the remaining balance in the account from which you borrowed is large enough for its intended purpose. Sweet, right?

You just need to be sure to account for all borrowing and transfers in the respective accounts.

Chapter Twenty-Seven

Reserve Accounts are also a good way to make your dreams come true. Our dreams are important and it is important to keep your dreams alive. The best way to keep a dream alive is to know that you are moving towards making it a reality; take a dream to see Paris in the spring, for example.

If all you do is dream about it, it is unlikely to ever come to pass. Of course, you can always charge the trip to a credit card but that can lead to feelings of guilt during the trip, remorse afterwards, and the hangover of debt for years to come. A better way to realize the dream is simply to budget for it using a Reserve Account.

If you figure the trip will cost $3,000 and you want to take it two years from now, all you do is divide the total cost by the number of months you have to get it funded by your target date. $3,000 divided by 24 months equals $125 a month.

If you don't have that amount in your budget, you now have the information you need to rearrange your finances. Either you reduce expenses elsewhere, if your dream is that compelling for you, or you extend your deadline from twenty-four months to, say, thirty months.

Or you get a second job or work overtime, whatever—with this information you can now (and probably for the first time!) exercise some real planning when it comes to achieving your dreams!

What before your Reserve Account was only a vague, unformed idea floating around in your head, is now a goal getting worked on paper and on its way to being realized. Before you had a hope, now you have a date to start packing!

Of course, the prudent use of credit in that example can also be justified. I don't want you to think that debt is some sort of boogeyman. Nothing could be farther from the truth.

Remember, I am The Debt Whisperer! You will never hear me raise my voice about the evils of debt. In fact, almost all of us will have occasion to use debt to finance a purchase at some point in our lives. Almost all of us, for example, will need a mortgage to finance the purchase of a home.

Also, many of us will need to get a loan to buy a car or pay for our education. Debt is a financial tool but it has gotten a bad reputation lately because too many of us have misused it and ended up in a financial mess.

In fact, the majority of us in the USA are not burdened with excessive consumer debt, contrary to what the press and a few financial pundits might lead you to believe. But, the other fact is, debt is a problem for more and more of us every year, as well!

If you want to take that trip to Paris and do not want to wait until you have the money saved to do so, charging the bill to a credit card could be entirely prudent depending on your particular circumstances. Certainly, you need to have enough room in your budget to pay off that bill in a reasonable amount of time.

The problem with using debt as a tactic to achieve your goal in this instance is that the interest charged on most credit cards will greatly inflate the actual cost of the trip over time.

For example, if you charge that entire $3,000 to a credit card charging 18% interest and pay that same $125 a month you were originally planning to save, you would end up paying a total of $3,750 for that $3,000 trip.

That is 25% more than the trip would have cost you had you had the cash to pay for it. Only you know if that trip is worth that amount to you or not.

But extend the payoff just one more year and the total will jump to a whopping $4,066 for that same Paris jaunt that was really only worth $3,000 to begin with!

Those figures reveal the problem with financing a purchase of any kind using debt. But, the thing is, some purchases warrant the added expense of interest on the debt. Managing your money will always be something of a balancing act. And, remember, your budget and your goals are both likely to change over time as your priorities shift.

The problem is that some people do not want to wait and save for anything—they want what they want right now! This want-it-now phenomenon is often referred to as the need for "instant gratification." The tendency towards wanting instant gratification of your wants is actually a sign of immaturity, although we can exhibit this tendency at any age.

Debt can be a prudent financial tool to use when the debt is secured and the object securing that debt is increasing in value. An example of a purchase made using debt but that is likely to increase in value is real estate, in particular, our primary residence. But, even in that instance, if you take thirty years to pay off your mortgage you should know that you will wind up paying almost three times the original cost of the house.

You can also justify the use of debt to purchase transportation and convenience in the form of a car or other vehicle. Again, the problem is when we use a tool in the wrong way and finance more car than we can actually afford.

But charging a meal to a credit card when you know you won't be able to pay the bill in full when it comes due is representative of how you can get into credit card debt and that sort of credit financing is difficult to justify and should be avoided. But for true needs such as a certain amount of vehicle financing and mortgage debt, credit can be a positive aspect of prudent financial planning.

In fact, based on my earlier discussion of the benefits of building a personal endowment, I do not recommend paying cash for cars or extra principal on your mortgage even if you can afford to until you have at least six months' worth of living expenses in savings.

And, even then, if the interest rate on your mortgage warrants it, I do not recommend paying off your mortgage in less than fifteen years because doing so will, necessarily be at the expense of building liquidity, that is, your cash reserves.

Most spending involves a trade-off. If we use it for this purpose, we can't use it for some other. Money used to pay down your mortgage balance cannot, then, be used to build your personal endowment.

Certainly, any extra amount you pay to your mortgage payment will have the effect of increasing your net worth (if the house is appreciating in value or, at least, not depreciating). And the money is not really spent as much as it is saved in the form of equity.

But equity is not liquid and houses do lose value. That being the case, equity can be a case of having too many eggs in one (not very liquid) basket.

Accelerating mortgage principal payments will save you money by decreasing the amount of interest you pay over the life of the loan. But those savings come at the cost of increased saving and the interest that would have been earned on those savings.

Afterword

Afterword

So, there you have it—The Plan, the thinking behind The Plan, and those additional strategies that will help you get what you want with the money you already have.

Just to recap:

It is more important that you are financially secure than it is that you are debt-free.

Money in the bank equals financial security.

Credit Card debt is a sign that you have been spending more than you earn.

Debt is just a symptom of the real problem—the real problem is spending more than you earn.

And last but not least, you must spend less than you earn in order to stop increasing your debt and to increase your savings.

I have watched my clients apply these strategies and achieve a higher level of financial security. And what has worked for them will, absolutely, work for you.

But your financial reality will not change until you do—the action required to realize your dreams is all up to you now.

So, in closing, let me just wish you good luck in your financial future and say thank you for reading my book—*The Debt Whisperer*—turning down the volume on the din of debt-reduction since 2007!

About the Author

Wallace R. Curiel is the author of several books, owner of Transcendental Media Group, and publisher of TMG Books and the website of the same name.

He is the owner of the trademark property:

The Debt Whisperer™

www.ingramcontent.com/pod-product-compliance
Lightning Source LLC
Chambersburg PA
CBHW051526170526
45165CB00002B/617